THE SEED THAT BECAME A GARDEN

The Seed That Became a Garden

The Story of Saint Marguerite Bourgeoys

Louise Finn, CND

Illustrations by Francis Back

ST PAULS

Library of Congress Cataloging-in-Publication Data

Finn, Louise.
  The seed that became a garden: the story of Saint Marguerite Bourgeoys / Louise
Finn, CND.
    pages cm
  Includes bibliographical references.
  ISBN 978-0-8189-1387-7
  1. Bourgeoys, Marguerite, Saint, 1620-1700. 2. Christian saints – Québec
(Province) – Biography. 3. Nuns – Québec (Province) – Biography. 4. Congregation
of Notre Dame – History – 17th century. 5. Montréal (Québec) – Church history – 17th
century. I. Title.
  BX4700.B77F56 2015
  271'.97 – dc23
  [B]   2015020105

Produced and designed in the United States of America by the
Fathers and Brothers of the Society of St. Paul,
2187 Victory Boulevard, Staten Island, New York 10314-6603
as part of their communications apostolate.

ISBN 978-0-8189-1387-7

Current Printing - first digit   1   2   3   4   5   6   7   8   9   1 0

Place of Publication:
2187 Victory Blvd., Staten Island, NY 10314 - USA

Year of Current Printing - first year shown

2015   2016   2017   2018   2019   2020   2021   2022   2023   2024

In gratitude to my family,
where seeds were planted and nourished with love, and
to my second family – Marguerite's garden,
where transplanted seedlings still thrive and flourish
in grace-full joy!

Contents

Foreword

In 1982 Marguerite Bourgeoys, a French woman of the seventeenth century, was "canonized," that is, officially declared a saint by the Church.

We may well ask, what can a person who lived more than three hundred years ago say to us today? In Marguerite's case, a great deal! She left her native France as a young, single lay woman to join with other committed lay persons in a magnificent adventure: to build a community of faith and charity in a small outpost in the New World. Today, in a world of global connections at every turn, we can still be challenged as Christians to allow our faith to shape our career choices and abandon nationalistic goals for the good of others in a distant land.

Marguerite committed herself to community-building within a society and Church which was itself not free from corruption or self-serving interests. Making and keeping a commitment was a challenge for her as it is for all of us today.

When the media portray the many sins of our Church today, the tendency is to equate the sins of the clergy or laity with the Body of Christ — to the exclusion of every other aspect of this Body. However, we are more than our sins; we are also our dreams. Marguerite was well aware of the difficulties of trying to do something new among those who fear change, for one person's vision can be a dangerous threat to others. Yet she dared to envision a new way of being Church.

There is still a cry among us for this vision, for this dream. Christians are still hoping that we as Church will respond in new ways to today's needs.

In New France Marguerite lived within a fort in a small village, but she went beyond its borders to the Native People, teaching their children and, in some cases, even opening special schools for them in their own villages. Today, walled neighborhoods have returned to our cities; fear keeps many behind the tall brick ramparts. The challenge today, as in Marguerite's time, is to go beyond the walls to be with *the others* — whoever these *others* may be. Walls in Texas and Arizona attempt to keep out the immigrant poor. Our faith challenges us to tackle the complexity of the immigrant issue with openness and charity.

Marguerite gathered women around her and eventually formed a religious community, the Congregation of Notre Dame. At a time when women religious were cloistered, she dreamed of a group that would follow the journeying Mother of God who went off to visit her cousin Elizabeth as soon as she heard that this elderly cousin was pregnant. Although Church authorities maintained that religious had to be cloistered, Marguerite continued the conversation about the possibility of another way.

In the pages that follow, you will learn more about this remarkable woman — in many respects, almost our contemporary.

In today's world, the soil in which our dreams are struggling to sprout is often dry and rocky. Tender seedlings are often cramped, drenched, shriveled, trampled or yanked up! With God's grace you will see new ways of meeting these challenges and living your Christian life.

Patricia McCarthy, CND

Introduction

Most plants begin as seeds. Rarely does a seed look like the plant it will become. Think of the mustard seed, the tiniest of seeds known to the farmers of Jesus' time, that becomes the mighty tree to "shelter the birds of the air" (*Matthew 13:31-32*).

Botanists tell us that a typical seed includes: (1) an embryo, or immature plant, (2) nutrients, and (3) a seed coat which protects the young plant. When the seed coat softens, the seed germinates, so that its embryo develops into a seedling, which then pushes above the soil into the air.

As it grows, most of the solid material in a plant is taken from the atmosphere. Through photosynthesis, plants use the energy in sunlight to convert carbon dioxide from the atmosphere, plus water, into simple sugars which then form the main structure of the plant. Mini-dramas, sheer poetry — and essential to our own lives! This book too began as a tiny seed, a strange response to reading Sr. Patricia McCarthy's little gem about Etty Hillesum.* It germinated

---

* *The Girl Who Learned to Kneel* (New York: Society of St. Paul, 2013)

in the rich soil of Sr. Patricia Simpson's two treasured volumes** about Saint Marguerite, and was nurtured by her helpful comments. Friends like Kevin Burns, Janet Kraus, Bill Schulz, Sisters Joyce Roberts, Ann Perrin and Louise Côté were its sunlight and moisture. My brother Ed and sister Chris cheered on its growth spurts, while my sister "Mickie," with her insightful questions, helped yank out some fuzzy weeds. Its beauty was enhanced by the exquisite illustrations of Francis Back, the historical artist who graciously allowed their use in this book. Marguerite herself kept it safe from predators. And, through the CND atmosphere around me, God supplied the energy to help it grow to fruition.

I am sincerely grateful to all, for all.

Louise Finn, CND

** Please see Bibliography.

1

The Soil

Marguerite Bourgeoys and her father in his candle workshop

$\mathcal{B}$e careful! Not too much moisture, or the seeds might rot or wash away; not too little, or they'll shrivel up and die! And soil not too hard and clumpy, or too soft and sandy. Not too cold either, or too hot. Sunshine? Of course — but not too much, or nights that are too long — or too short! The gardener knows all this — and more! — about finding the *right* soil for her precious plants. As incredible as it may seem, God has chosen the *right* (not perfect, but right) soil — family, nation, century, everything! — for each of us, for you and for me.

But this book is about Marguerite Bourgeoys, not about us (at least, not directly). Her life began in 1619. She was born in April 1620, in Troyes, France. What kind of soil was hers? As the seventh child in a middle-class family, this soil must have been charged with fertile energy, since six more children arrived after Marguerite. Her father, Abraham Bourgeoys, had a steady job as a candle-maker — perhaps considered essential services back then. He was also one of the city's Mint officers, a title bordering on nobility. Judging from the items left in his will twenty-three years later, the family was not poor. However, they no doubt all pitched in with the household chores, especially with meal preparation and clean-up. Marguerite was evidently healthy, surviving several epidemics that swept through Troyes during her childhood — the probable cause of the deaths of three of the younger children. When she was eighteen, her mother died rather suddenly, perhaps from complications in a late pregnancy. In any case, Marguerite's young years were not without their sad and difficult moments.

Like most middle-class children at that time, Marguerite was probably enrolled in the school run by the cloistered sisters in the city of Troyes. These must have been both enjoyable and successful experiences, for she later wrote about the joy she felt at gathering other youngsters — siblings and neighbors, no doubt — to "teach" them too. "From early childhood, God had given me the inclination to gather little girls of my own age together to live and work together in some distant place to earn our living." (*Writings of Marguerite Bourgeoys,* p. 162, and hereafter: *Writings*)

Her words are few — their point being God's work within her even as a child, but in light of her later work, both in Troyes and in New France, they are too tempting to resist as the basis for imagined scenes. Stained glass picture-windows in the city's churches — all rich in devotional art, would provide visual aids for her Bible lessons, as well as safe destinations for their field trips. Even as a child, she must have felt at home in God's house.

Indeed, in many ways Christian faith permeated the activities of the time. In fact, when Marguerite was only one day old, she was taken to the nearby church to be baptized. As she grew, she was surrounded not only by the younger children, but by loving parents and her caring older brothers and sisters. From this nurturing atmosphere she imbibed the strong values that shaped her strong character. In many ways she was a typical adolescent — fun-loving and fashion-conscious. However, in the absence of the many sources of entertainment which sometimes clutter our own use of time, Marguerite turned almost naturally to wholesome pursuits — no batteries needed (or available back then).

Like children everywhere, Marguerite's heart was being shaped by the people and events in her early years. Were all these influences — her family, friends and relatives, her native city and parish church in the seventeenth century — part of God's plan to help this young, outgoing, cheerful personality develop into an attractive and responsible leader? Most certainly.

As a "middle child," Marguerite had a variety of role models to study, evaluate and emulate, as well as a number of younger "sibs" to interact with (and practice on!) in her emerging maturity. The spirituality that she encountered in those around her was neither stifling nor austere, and was untouched by the rising taint of Jansenism which saw evil lurking in every corner. On the contrary, from the loving atmosphere in her home, her caring teachers at school, and the saints depicted in church statues, the spirituality she breathed in was down-to-earth, relational, practical and life-giving!

It was time for God to plant the seed.

2

The Seed

Marguerite Bourgeoys, Prefect of the "Congrégation
Externe de Notre-Dame" in Troyes, France

$\mathcal{A}$s a teenager — though the term was not used at the time, Marguerite was popular with her "crowd." Some of them belonged to the group that met regularly at the cloistered sisters' convent in Troyes. At that time (as well as today), being cloistered meant that these sisters had chosen to live their lives of prayer and good works within their convent walls. To support themselves, they conducted a school inside the convent. Their school was noted for the quality of the teachers whose methods were considered quite advanced in the early 1600s.

At that time too, the city of Troyes was losing its luster in both its wealth and its population. It had once been prosperous, situated at the crossroads of trade routes, famous for its poets and merchants. When things are named after you, you are clearly thought to be important. And this is also true of places. The city's name lives on in the measure used for precious metals and gemstones — Troy weight. In the 1600s, however, almost one-third of its families were poor, and since there were no free public schools, for these families educating their children was not an option.

To their credit, these cloistered sisters, the *Congrégation de Notre-Dame* (Our Lady's Congregation), came up with a way to help the poor families of the city who could not afford schooling for their children: they started an outreach group of about thirty young women. The sisters first taught the members of this group, which they called an "Extern Congregation," their own teaching techniques. The women then used these same methods to conduct classes for the poor children wherever they could find places to meet. Great symbiosis!

Marguerite had not joined this Extern Congregation, probably because their "dress code" seemed too showy, or dramatic, or perhaps this code was simply too difficult for her to accept at this point in her life: dresses that were too plain and old-fashioned, *and* worst of all, no jewelry or fancy lace! Over and over they invited her, but to no avail. However, this was soon to change.

In Troyes at this time, an important part of parish life was the custom of prayerful processions, held either inside the church building, or spilling over into the nearby cobblestoned streets. Such an overflow occurred during the procession on the Feast of the Rosary, October 7, 1640. Marguerite, who had just turned twenty, was part of the large crowd walking in prayer to honor Mary, and was unaware that a life-changing experience was about to occur in her heart.

In telling about this experience later, Marguerite never implied that she had an apparition or a vision. She simply wrote, "I was strongly moved when I looked up at the statue of the Blessed Virgin (on the outer wall of the church). I found it very beautiful. At the same time, I found myself so moved that I no longer recognized myself." (*Writings*, p. 163)

God — and Mary — had planted the seed within Marguerite's heart.

She later also recounted that when she returned home, her family too noticed the change — no doubt because she offered all her lace collars and fine jewelry to her sisters, thrilled at their new treasures. Yes, she had decided to take the first steps to joining the Extern Congregation, so there was no point in her keeping them.

Before making such a decisive move, Marguerite — wise woman that she was even in her youth, thoroughly investigated this group. She was now exploring her world with new eyes, and with a healthy and attentive mind. She soon realized that the educational philosophy of the cloistered sisters, which they were sharing with their outreach Extern group, was consonant with her own. Not only were these sisters experienced and advanced in their methods, but their motivation was sound. They saw in the children whom they taught God's own daughters and the future mothers of families who would one day wield great influence over their own children. They realized too that even their present families would benefit from these youngsters' education. Marguerite deeply desired to help these young girls to *understand*, an intrinsic goal of all true education.

The sisters also shared Marguerite's conviction that the needs of the poor — the many poor in Troyes — were God's way of calling her to act. So act she did, joining the

Extern Congregation of Notre Dame of Troyes. Her friends, of course, were delighted. She was so *present* to each event and each person in her life! Gentle and affable too, and sensitive to the needs of both her colleagues and those to whom they were ministering — hundreds of students and, in some cases, their families too.

Moreover, Marguerite's keen mind was able to envision the next step while most were struggling to focus on the task at hand. With clarity and conviction, she could present new ideas without threatening those who preferred the old ways. (Even Jesus had to deal with the hostility of those who resented the ways he socialized with outcasts.) With the devastation and poverty she now saw around her, Marguerite's heart was growing in compassion and, as if on fire with God's love for humankind, she brought this love to her world.

Can we be surprised that soon Marguerite was elected president of the group? Within the next few years, their numbers increased from thirty to more than four hundred!

Yet, this seed within her was reaching up in another direction; another desire was forming within this searching heart.

3

The Seedling

$\mathcal{A}$ sprouting seed needs nurturing soil. From the moment Marguerite saw Mary in a new light during the Rosary procession, she had felt encompassed by God's love, by Mary's smile. Her desire to give herself completely to God never wavered, and she now considered entering one of the cloistered religious communities in Troyes. With the approval of her confessor, Father Gendret, to whom she had opened her heart, she applied to the Carmelites and asked permission to join them. However, they refused. Why? We don't know, but it perhaps had to do with the number of sisters already in the convent — no extra space for new ones. She also considered another cloistered community, but that too did not work out. Both of these events must have been deeply disappointing, as well as confusing. Rejection is never easy.

Although Marguerite's membership in the Extern Congregation played an important role during the next decade, she never felt that this was to become her life's work. Father Gendret, who knew her well and was aware that she was old enough to choose not to marry, approved of her making private vows of poverty and chastity. This was a custom for some individuals at the time, as it still is — though much less frequently today. At least it must have given Marguerite a sense of moving forward.

Some people can see in their own mental landscape farther than others can see in theirs. Father Gendret must have been one such person, and he must have sensed that Marguerite was too. Having witnessed her successful leadership as a member of the extern group, he suggested that she begin her *own* religious community, one that would *not* be cloistered, but would combine a life of prayer with apostolic action. A bold initiative, to say the least, but one that Marguerite was willing to try.

With her customary energy and openness, she approached two other young women with similar motivation, and they soon began the experiment. Their house-hunting was resolved when a "friend of a friend" offered them a place to rent in Troyes. Many a discussion must have followed as they planned the practical aspects of their life together — prayer schedule, meals, housecleaning, food shopping, and the rest, all this, while continuing their various ministries. No doubt she missed a few days of her outreach to the poor, but their new "community" finally began!

As their model, they chose Mary's life, both during Jesus' years of teaching and healing, as well as after his death and resurrection. As the Gospels tell us, Mary was not cloistered but was often with the women who were ministering to Jesus' needs and those of his followers. The *Acts of the Apostles* also portrays Mary as integral to the early Church, no doubt encouraging the apostles in their efforts to spread the Good News of God's love for humankind.

This was the kind of religious community that Marguerite and her two companions were trying to be: nourished by their life of prayer together and going out to both men and women, wherever they were needed, as Mary did. They saw Mary "where the action was" — at simple ceremonies in the Temple, at wedding feasts, at the coming of the Spirit in the Upper Room. Perhaps they also spoke of Mary's awareness at Cana that the embarrassing wine shortage might well have been caused by Jesus' thirsty apostles.

Marguerite would have been familiar with the wall sculpture in her parish church depicting the Visitation — Mary embracing Elizabeth, her pregnant cousin. That was the way saints were depicted at the time, not alone (that style was to come later), but in relationship with at least one other person.

As Marguerite understood the way the followers of Jesus spread the word in the decades following his Ascension, both men and women instructed others in the new faith. This understanding may have been rooted in the position of women during medieval times in her native city, where some women had exerted great power in civil or Church society. For example, in previous centuries the abbess of a monastery of women ("monasteries" may house a group of either men or women) might have more authority than the local bishop. Although this unusual situation regarding women had changed, perhaps Marguerite had inherited its spirit. She was certainly a strong personality, a woman of strength, able and willing to walk new paths within a traditional Church. She and her companions were testing the waters.

However, this new form of religious life was not to be. Marguerite later wrote — without going into detail, that one of the young women died, and the other decided to leave. Surely Marguerite was again deeply saddened and disappointed, but continued her work in the Extern Congregation among the poor, teaching the children and helping their families.

Working thus among the poor was not without its dangers. At this time in France, Catholics and Protestants were often in conflict — the so-called Religious Wars, with their concomitant threats and risks. Moreover, the political unrest in Troyes was such that laws had been passed ordering beggars to leave the city by sundown, under penalty of imprisonment. Citizens were even forbidden to help the poor directly. Instead, benefactors were to give to the institutions established for that purpose. Moreover, dangers of contagion and violence lurked in the city's outskirts where the poor were housed — the wealthy and middle class being ensconced in the inner-city. No doubt Marguerite's family were concerned about her safety, but she and her companions seemed to have been spared any serious mishaps.

Even if we have suffered mishaps, serious or otherwise (and who of us hasn't?), psychologists tell us that no experience in our life is ever really wasted. We can grow into the person we were meant to be either because of *or* in spite of these events. As St. Paul said, "All things work together for good for those who love God" (*Romans 8:28*). It had now been twelve years since Marguerite had experienced Mary's "smile" during the Rosary procession, when she must have felt — and *known* — God's unconditional love for her through his mother's gaze. She had responded to this love as fully as she could, developing into a woman of deep, active faith and loving trust, ready to follow the voice of her God as soon as she heard even a whisper. Her daily efforts to do so were surely *true leaves* on the young plant.

4

Time to Transplant?

Sister Louise de Maisonneuve introduces Marguerite
to her brother Paul during his visit to Troyes.

$\mathcal{G}$ardeners know that transplanting seedlings is a tricky process. The roots must be strong enough to adapt to the new soil, which, in turn must be compatible to their needs — moderate moisture, plenty of minerals and other nutrients. Temperatures must not differ drastically from the original habitat, lest the little plant die of shock. Periods of light and darkness must be conducive to growth.

They also know that the stem must have "true leaves," sturdy enough to be handled safely. Marguerite's activities during this decade — including at least one apparent failure — were surely these *true leaves*. Soon she would be called to become part of a new endeavor: to cross the Atlantic and help *found a city in the New World!*

To understand the conditions — and dangers — that Marguerite would soon be facing, a few historical facts are needed here. The idea for founding the city of Ville-Marie on the banks of the St. Lawrence River in present-day Canada seems to have originated in the 1630s. More than just another trading post, the city of Quebec had managed to retain its position as a permanent settlement since Champlain's group of about two dozen had wintered there in 1608. However, by establishing the fur trade, Champlain had allied the French with the Algonquins and the Hurons, thus making them (the French) enemies of the Iroquois, or Five Nations. What we now know as Canada was a battleground for colonial powers. The French claimed it, but the British wanted it and fought for it — sometimes by providing arms to their trading partners, the Iroquois. These, in turn, had attacked and killed many bands of Algonquins. Many of these latter had also been decimated by a series of epidemics. Besides being friendly to the French, the Algonquins had served as a barrier against the hostile Iroquois. Many mishaps — and tragedies! — awaited the small band of "colonists" preparing to found Ville-Marie, the city we know today as Montreal.

In the 1600s an ocean voyage to the New World was high-risk travel for passengers and crew alike. Sailing vessels were subject to possible attack by enemy ships, tossed about by gale-force winds, becalmed for days — or even weeks. All on board, meanwhile, would endure at least a month of discomfort and often starvation-rations. Yet in 1641 the soldiers and recruits for Ville-Marie finally set sail from France on two different ships. In charge of the first was the man who was the leader of the expedition and governor of the new colony, Paul de Chomedey de Maisonneuve. Because of poor weather and the state of his vessel, he had had to return to port three times, and in the process had lost not only two weeks' sailing time, but also four of his recruits. The other ship, with Jeanne Mance in charge (more about her later), was first to arrive in the village of Quebec, where they would all have to spend the winter before moving on in the spring. During these months the Quebec colonists tried desperately to persuade the settlers from both ships to stay — not from friendly motives, but simply to have more able-bodied men to defend their own colony. In early May of 1642, however, the new settlers (about forty in number) finally left Quebec, sailed up the St. Lawrence River, and ten days later arrived in Montreal.

The next decade can be summed up in two brief, stark phrases: stagnation and guerilla warfare with the Iroquois. After nine years of seemingly hopeless struggles, in 1651 de Maisonneuve returned to France on family business, as well as to recruit more colonists.

Such was the situation that awaited these colonists.

When de Maisonneuve arrived in Troyes, he visited his sister Louise, the cloistered sister who directed the Extern Congregation. Although these nuns had hoped to become part of the new colony, de Maisonneuve realized that, given the primitive conditions in the colony, this would be impossible. However, he did ask his sister if she knew anyone who could join them and become the teacher — when there would finally be children to teach.

Without a moment's hesitation Louise recommended Marguerite. We can almost hear her enthusiastic words: *Brother Paul, have I got the perfect person for your new colony! She's courageous, filled with faith and common sense, healthy, generous, a born leader and a great teacher!* At their meeting soon after, both de Maisonneuve and Marguerite must have felt similar vibes: *Yes, I could work with her. Yes, I sense that he can be trusted.* Before giving her final answer, Marguerite stepped back a bit to ponder, pray and consult.

Marguerite's younger siblings were now adults and her dear father had died, so no family obligations held her back. Although women at this time were not thought of as having "careers," teaching seemed to be her true calling — she loved it and did it well. Fr. Gendret even suggested that perhaps, although their plan to begin a non-cloistered religious community had not succeeded in Troyes, in God's providence it might well succeed in New France. In her heart Marguerite knew that the poor in Troyes would not be abandoned if she left; many other young women would continue working with them. Yes, it was settled. She would go to Ville-Marie.

Between Marguerite's decision to go and her actual departure lay a series of obstacles, each one an acid test of her mettle. An attractive woman traveling alone to the port city caused more than raised eyebrows. Not being allowed to take a room in the inns along the way was only one of the insults, misunderstandings and rebuffs Marguerite encountered. Perhaps the most perplexing, however, came from a most unexpected source.

Shortly before she was to embark on the ship, Marguerite received word from the Carmelites that she could now enter any one of their convents. This had been her dream from her earliest days after Mary had touched her heart during the Rosary procession. Would she be turning her back on God's invitation if she now walked away — or sailed away? As always, she prayed mightily and consulted carefully. She later wrote that, in the morning, when she was fully awake, a tall woman in white serge spoke plainly to her, saying, "Go, I will never abandon you." (*Writings*, p. 165) She knew it was Mary, and again at peace, continued on her journey.

And what a journey! Two months at sea in a disease-ridden ship (a mere fraction of the size and tonnage of our ocean liners), with no doctor, nurse or priest aboard. Marguerite became all three, tending the sick, comforting the dying, and praying over the eight who died en route. No doubt de Maisonneuve realized more and more each day the treasure he had in this young woman, and thanked God each night that both of them had — so far! — survived the voyage.

Finally, at long last, land! Alleluia! Like the earlier colonists, their first stop was Quebec, where they unloaded supplies which were meant for the mother colony, and allowed the exhausted sailors and recruits to rest and recuperate. It was here that Marguerite gave her own mattress to a fellow-traveler who was cold and ill. Transplanted, her new life had begun!

5

The New Soil

Marguerite and some helpers working at the Stable-School
during a visit by Governor Paul de Maisonneuve

$\mathcal{D}$espite the shock involved to a young transplant, if it's strong and healthy enough, it can survive. Marguerite was both hardy and resilient. She knew how to adapt, how to tap into her inner resources, how to reach out to others, both to help them when she could and to receive sustenance for her own human needs.

During the challenges of basic survival in these early years, as well as during the more subtle difficulties that arose later, she and her two friends, Jeanne Mance, the director of the colony's primitive "hospital," and Paul de Maisonneuve, the leader and governor, were surely each other's chief support. They seem to have been a wholesome trio — able to be close without trying to possess or control the other two. All three were evidently mature enough to enjoy and appreciate their friendship as *pure gift!*

However, without enough children in the colony to warrant opening a school, what was Marguerite to do all day? Any mother would laugh at that question, and Marguerite was truly the Mother of Ville-Marie. Besides being the village catechist, sacristan, liturgist and choir director, no doubt she served as tutor, baby-sitter, marriage counselor, psychologist, hospital helper, seamstress, nutrition consultant, nurse-practitioner, leader of sing-alongs and referee-on-call, the go-to-person on duty, on deck. No wonder she could later urge her sisters to "become skilled in all kinds of work"! All this was her way, for the time being, of living the *"Vie Voyagère"* of Mary — traveling, like Mary, to whoever needed her help. (The literal translation, "Journeying Life," needs to be nuanced. Marguerite used this phrase to describe the manner in which Mary — and therefore she and her sisters — would go out to others, traveling anywhere to do good.)

It's surely impossible for us to imagine how different this new soil must have been for Marguerite after her three decades in Troyes. The village of Ville-Marie was still an outpost; the colonists' safety lay within the small fort. Those who dared to hunt or farm in the surrounding forests or fields ran the risk of being brutally murdered. We can only try to picture everyday activities, both in the scorching heat of summer and in the long, dark, frigid winters. Rutted pathways when the ice melted, pitiful harvests when the rains came late — or didn't come at all. Running out of flour months before the ships from France could arrive again in late spring. Racking coughs that kept everyone in the small houses (*and* their neighbors) awake all night, and carried some off to the small but growing cemetery. All this and more, much more!

Surely she felt one big difference between her native France and its new colony: almost everyone in Ville-Marie had *chosen* to be there. The colonists' motives, in themselves, constituted a rather incredible story.

Ville-Marie — the City of Mary — with its unusual name and inspiration for its founding, dated back to at least

1640. Although virtually all human endeavors spring from a variety of mixed motivations, these founders expressed explicitly in their documents their desire to *help the native peoples by founding a community in which they would live like the first Christians, so that they could share with these "benighted" people their most prized possession — their Christian faith.* To us, this may sound completely unreal, but their original motives are well documented by competent historians.

In its early stages, the founding of Ville-Marie was envisioned, planned and carried out, not by government officials or royalty, but by ordinary lay men and women. This group later broadened to include clergy and nobles, and the early inhabitants included middle-class workers and orphan girls, paid soldiers and volunteer artisans. In many ways the settlement was inspired by the first Jesuit mission in New France. This mission, probably begun to create "new" France in the colonies, its founders driven by both religious and economic motivations, apparently became the victim of conflicts between English and French merchants and traders. Although the mission itself seemed to have failed rather miserably, elements of its brief history (1611-1614) reappeared in the founding of Ville-Marie. Moreover, in God's good time, another fruit of the Jesuits' fine labor would appear in Marguerite's life.

While waiting for the children to be sufficient in number and old enough for Marguerite to start a school, she undertook one major project dear to her heart: the building of a church. It was to be small by our standards, but large enough to accommodate all the colonists. She began, of course, by seeking ecclesiastical permission, which she obtained. Next, probably in consultation with de Maison-neuve, she chose the perfect location — beside the St. Law-rence River. No doubt they envisioned the statue of *Notre Dame de Bon Secours* (Our Lady, Help of Christians) atop its steeple, welcoming the weary sailors on their arrival in Ville-Marie, Mary's own city.

For the construction itself, she sought the help of the men of the town, most of whom were still bachelors. In re-turn for a day's labor, she would do whatever sewing or mending they needed done. They happily agreed — felling and dragging trees for the framework, gathering stones for the building itself. For two years the work progressed slowly but well, until in 1657 it was interrupted.

The reasons for this were a sorry combination of Church politics and conflicting views about the purpose of the settlers' presence and work in French Canada. Unan-swered questions like: "*Who* is in charge in this colony?" and "Are we here to build 'The City of God' *or* to build a viable economy?" affected major decisions. Both questions were rooted in European connections, and both were valid goals on their own terms, but their competing motivations caused havoc in the colony.

An obvious example of this occurred when Marguerite was ordered by the new Vicar General to stop building the church. She obeyed, trusting that if God wanted it finished, finished it would be — in God's good time. Marguerite knew how to obey and how to wait.

In some ways, the mid-1650s were years of relative peace — if not within the Church community, at least with the Iroquois. At long last it seemed relatively safe to open a school outside the fort. An empty building, available because it was no longer used, was chosen and officially deeded to Marguerite. The first floor was to be the schoolroom for the girls, while the dove-cote above would be the residence for Marguerite and the other women — whenever more teachers would be needed. At night, for safety's sake, they would draw up the outside ladder into the area where they slept.

One major problem, however, had to be taken care of before they could move in. The building had been vacant for about five years, and its original inhabitants had been cattle. Cows? Oh no-o-o! Oh yes, it was definitely a stable in every imaginable way. With her customary energy and with the help of the students (and of some parents, we hope), Marguerite was able to remove, or at least diminish, the most distinctive traces of the previous occupants. In the midst of this backbreaking and unpleasant task, surely the significance of her new work being born in a stable was not lost on Marguerite. On April 30, 1658, teacher and pupils moved in to Montreal's first public school. Her dream was becoming reality!

For the next five months (or perhaps fewer, if the summer heat was too enervating), the schoolroom buzzed with happy activity. Yet another interruption was waiting in the wings: her friend Jeanne Mance, so vital to the community both as general treasurer and as founder/director of the small hospital, had broken her right arm. Her constant pain and inability to function made it clear that she must get to France to see if her arm could be treated and healed. Jeanne would not be able to make this voyage alone, so Marguerite arranged to travel with her.

Fortunately, one of the wrinkles of the messy Church politics mentioned above was the arrival in Montreal of two "good hospital nuns" (actually sent from Quebec to *displace* Jeanne). What to do with these fine women, caught in the ecclesiastical crossfire? Marguerite tactfully arranged for them to replace her as teacher during her trip to France. In mid-October, 1658, Jeanne and Marguerite finally left on one of the last ships to sail that year, leaving behind the "new soil," now no longer new, but more like their new home!

6

Growth Spurts

Marguerite and new companions embark for New France
on the St. André.

*L*ife's mishaps often lead to unexpected blessings, especially if we maintain a positive attitude, which Marguerite surely did. Once the ailing Jeanne was safely in the caring hands of her sister in Paris, Marguerite was free to pursue another reason for returning to France. Where did she go? To Troyes, of course! After having been away for almost six years, it must have been a culture shock in reverse to be once again in safe neighborhoods with cobbled streets, in huge churches filled with all kinds of art works, and most of all, in warm homes with loving family and friends. Some had died, and grief was tangible. Some had grown from babies to teenagers, or so it seemed. Louise de Maisonneuve, of course, listened with rapt interest to stories of her younger brother Paul's adventures — relief, pride and gratitude shining in her eyes. Though Marguerite wrote very little about her own family, no doubt she visited them, soaking up every moment of every visit.

But soon she addressed her deepest hope in returning to Troyes — to seek helpers to go back to Ville-Marie with her. And where did she first turn? Where else but to her friends and associates in the Extern Congregation. Three young women caught her enthusiasm and immediately said yes! Catherine Crolo had wanted to join Marguerite back in 1653, and later became the physical backbone of the early group as she managed the farm that kept them alive. Edmée Chastel's story had a rather comic twist. With tearful hesitation her father let her go, insisting that she secretly sew some gold coins into her corset (which all women wore back then) for her ship's passage in case she ever wanted to return. Edmee never did need the money, and eventually gave it to Marguerite. The third was Marie Raisin, still in her twenties, still filled with the *joie-de-vivre* of the young! To each of them she promised only bread and soup, and a hard life as they earned their keep so as to teach the children without cost. When they reached Paris on their way to meet Jeanne Mance — now healed! — a fourth recruit, Anne Hiou, came forward and was gladly accepted.

All this may sound idyllic. A successful quest and a happy ending to a difficult journey. But the journey was not over. Carriage drivers exacted extra fares for their work, and at the last minute the ship's captain raised the rates for all passengers. Somehow Marguerite and Jeanne found ways to deal with these monetary crises. However, some strange rumors began circulating that this group of people bound for New France had been kidnapped and were going there against their will. Bands of townspeople surrounded the area to "protect" them from being put on the ship. Probably with a show of force, the milling crowd — about two hundred, including the crew — were at last safely on board — or so they thought.

An ocean voyage in the 1600s was uncomfortable, to say the least. More truthfully, it was fraught with dangers of every kind — weather, tainted food (or no food), capture by enemy ships, living in extremely close quarters with total strangers for several months — the actual length of time depending on the winds. Marguerite and her four companions expected all this, but soon found out that even worse awaited them: their ship, the *St. André*, had served as a hospital ship for the military, and was still germ-infested.

Shortly after they left port, the plague broke out. Almost everyone on board became ill, some so seriously that they were bedridden for the entire voyage — among them Jeanne Mance who, as an experienced nurse, could have helped had she been well enough. As it was, Marguerite and her new recruits pitched in, encouraging the fearful, tending the sick, comforting the dying; consequently, except for brief moments of respite, finding time to pray as a group was probably a low priority. Approximately ten people were buried at sea. This was not a pleasure cruise.

In early September they landed in Quebec, where some stayed behind to recuperate. Marguerite and the rest — including her four new "sisters," went on to Montreal. As they traveled upriver, she was surely happy to point out their Stable-School, then farther along near the dock where they landed, even the pitiful fort must have been a welcome sight.

What a strange beginning for Marguerite's little community! The five had set sail on the feast of Mary's Visitation, and had spent these first months together, but were also side-by-side with the other dozen women on board. The five had reached out to serve where they were needed, doing the most menial of tasks. In Marguerite's mind, her new community had been born, had undergone its first test, and had survived. The second half of her dream was becoming reality, and not merely surviving, but growing! A grateful Alleluia rose from her tired heart.

7

Standing "on its Own"

Faced with shortages of fabric in New France, a Sister of Marguerite
Congregation teaches young women to make cloth themselves.

*W*hy the quotation marks around "on its Own" in the title of this chapter? So often we think we are in charge, but God is sustaining us in all that we do. "Unless the Lord builds the house, they labor in vain who build it" (*Psalm 127:1*). Marguerite knew this as she surveyed the colony on her return. Had the Stable-School, the small seedling, also survived? Had the colony changed in the two years since she had left with Jeanne Mance? Yes, to both. However, Marguerite saw with sadness that all the materials that had been gathered for the Church of Bon Secours had disappeared — scattered here and there. She turned her energies to the school, where all five women now lived their daily life in a single room downstairs. Though it had a fireplace and chimney, it offered little comfort. Nor was there any privacy in the common bedroom upstairs. Moreover, the beautiful nearby forests could not be used for a brief get-away, since the dangers of Iroquois raids still lurked outside the fort. Even their own house was probably considered a public building, open to all whenever needed, for meetings or ceremonies, or as a get-away place for *other* people!

And what of the evenings and nights? If water in a pitcher on their table froze within fifteen minutes during a winter day, it's hard to imagine how they were ever able to work at night. Yet the sewing, mending and patching of clothes had to be done, since it brought in the money they needed to support their teaching. At least Sister Crolo — hard-working and congenial Catherine — was able to take care of all the laundry they took in. Besides all this, with the increased number of families and children, their school was soon to outgrow this building.

But first, Marguerite needed to turn her attention to another group of settlers that had begun to arrive: the *"filles du roi."* These were not really "daughters (or girls) of the king" as the name implies, but young women from France who agreed to come to the new colony as prospective wives and mothers. These King's Wards were probably orphans, unable to supply the dowry required for an honorable marriage, and this new arrangement would be their path to a better life.

As soon as Marguerite heard of this new government policy (which lasted only ten years), she undoubtedly knew what she would have to do: not only be at the dock to welcome these young women, but actually *stay with them* until they found suitable husbands among the bachelors — and Marguerite knew that *that* should not be rushed!

The first group of King's Wards were seventeen in number. Two years later came another group of eleven, and finally, in 1668, thirteen more. At the beginning they shared the upstairs living quarters with the small community, drawing the outside ladder up each night, but this living arrangement would *never* work out long-term. Marguerite had bought a house that was available, and arranged to use it for their new home. To make it a true home for these young women, it would need — *they* would need! — a mother. Without hesitation, she moved in with them, though she was aware that her sisters (they were now using that word to designate members of the group) were not happy with this move. But what else could she do, since, as she later wrote, this was for the sake of *families!* (*Writings*, p. 178)

Seemingly, these young women needed to learn just about everything — which plants were edible and which were poisonous, how to prepare a savory meal from unsavory ingredients, how to heat a house safely — with enough ventilation *and* without burning it down, how to bake bread that would not double as ammunition. In short, "Survival 101." Even more important perhaps, Marguerite helped some of them choose just the right husband, and was there for them after their first spat, or after a miscarriage, or saddest of all, at the death of a dear child.

For many, Marguerite was the mother they had never known. And as she learned to play her new role, she gradually helped the young women to feel at home in this strange land. They were members of Marguerite's family, part of her flourishing plant.

Yet, they were surrounded by other dangers. Iroquois raids and brave acts of resistance continued. Several years of famine resulted from the settlers' not being able to farm outside the fort. The colony's fur trade suffered when Algonquin canoes laden with pelts were unable to get past the Iroquois — a harsh blow to the fragile economy of New France.

During this decade too, the political and ecclesiastical scenes in the colony were changing. The complications of both are far beyond the scope of this book, but their results might be summed up: Although "new" Montreal was on a stronger footing militarily and economically, some of its inhabitants were no longer striving to live like the early Christians. For them, the founders' original vision — its *raison d'être* — had been lost.

Marguerite, of course, was fully aware of this change, and without lowering her standards of either education or religious life, she adapted. Bishop Laval was urging her to expand their teaching throughout the entire colony of New France. Making the rounds of all the settlements in the growing diocese of Quebec, with so few sisters, was impossible — since it stretched from the Atlantic, along both sides of the St. Lawrence, across the Great Lakes, through the Midwest down to New Orleans. But they did their best. The young plant was thriving.

8

Darkness and Light

Sister Thérèse Gannensagoua and a teaching companion at
the Mountain Mission

*T*oo much darkness could cause the young plant to wither, as could too much sunlight. Throughout Marguerite's life both seemed to be evenly distributed. For example, she must have often wondered if Bon Secours Chapel would *ever* be finished! More than twenty years after it had been interrupted, she still longed for the day when people could come in pilgrimage to visit Our Lady's shrine. Meanwhile, she knew that surely Mary was watching over the growing settlement. During her previous voyage to France, the materials gathered with so much effort had disappeared; before she left on her next trip, she built a small wooden oratory in its place, so that the site itself would not be given away.

Yes, in 1670 Marguerite made another journey back to France. Realizing that she would soon need legal authorization for her community to teach in the colony, once more she faced the long ocean voyage. However, this time her small parcel of luggage was somehow left behind! Since she was the only woman on board, she probably spent most of the voyage on the salt-sprayed deck, and for bedding made do with some coarse sail-cloth and a coil of rope. She thanked God that the trip had lasted "only 31 days." (*Writings*, p. 37)

Her first stop was in Paris, where she visited her old friend Paul de Maisonneuve. She had not seen him since he had returned to France "on family business" five years before. Their meeting must have been bittersweet, eagerly exchanging news of each other and the colony, yet painfully aware of the poor treatment he had received before leaving the city to which he had given his very life's blood. As always, he helped Marguerite in every way possible, arranging to replace the missing documents in her small satchel still in Quebec, and taking care of her immediate financial needs.

Of course, she next went to her native Troyes, giving news of her companions to their families, and visiting her own. Three of her nieces seemed to share Marguerite's adventure-gene and eagerly asked to return with her, as did five other young women in the city. In all she signed contracts with six of these who wished to become part of her new community. These new recruits would more than double the size of her group.

Upon her return to New France in 1672, it must have been heart-rending for Marguerite to see that the health of her dear friend Jeanne Mance was in serious decline. She died the following year. Within two years Governor de Maisonneuve also died in France; Marguerite was to be the last of the original threesome of the early days. Both Jeanne and Paul were in their mid-sixties; she herself was 55 and — interesting to note — ten years beyond the average lifespan of most people of her time.

Life goes on, they say, and so it did. In 1676 the sisters opened two "missions" in nearby villages where the sisters would not only teach, but also live. The first was a school for the children in an Indian settlement close to Ville-Marie. To make the children feel more at home, the two sisters lived in a bark hut — as did all the Indian settlers — with a fire in the center and a hole at the top for the escaping smoke. Not long after, two young Native women from this mission (one a Mohawk-Huron and the other an Iroquois) joined the Congregation, as Marguerite's group was now called, and went to the village to teach the people. The Mohawk-Huron sister was Gannensagoua, whose grandfather had been among those baptized by Jean de Brébeuf at the Jesuit mission mentioned earlier. (Although this mission was closed in 1614 after three short years, had it really been a failure? As she watched young Gannensagoua starting off eagerly for the Mountain Mission, Marguerite surely knew that the Jesuits' hard and dangerous work had borne rich fruit!) This Mountain Mission, the first beyond the island of Montreal, also had to be closed a few years later, no doubt occasions for Marguerite of both light and darkness — the rhythm of life.

9

Slugs and Snails

Following the tragic fire, Marguerite and her sisters
search through the remains.

*Y*oung plants are often attacked by other creatures. Growth is often painful, and Marguerite's community was growing. In fact, it was now in its "institutionalization" phase, with the inevitable struggles to adapt to larger numbers without losing its original vision. Their goal of living a poor life, like that of the girls and women whom they taught, raised practical questions for the group. Should they really have built a large house when the Stable School and its addition became too inconvenient for all involved? This last issue especially seemed to be at the root of Marguerite's *mental anguish* (her own words) when she decided, in 1680, to return once more to France. The trip would also give her an opportunity to study the "Rules" of two new un-cloistered communities, in preparation for writing her own Rule for the Congregation.

After a comparatively uneventful voyage — no epidemic, no deaths or fires onboard, no enemy ships encountered, and finally, a safe arrival, Marguerite was able to speak with a Franciscan priest in France, and was once again at peace. However, her next encounter was less than pleasant. When she visited Bishop Laval in Paris, he himself was under great stress because of clashes between Church policies and state politics. His response to her visit was far from welcoming. In fact, perhaps because he wanted to avoid having to deal with one more set of problems, his solution might have sounded like this:

Sister Marguerite, I have given much prayer and thought to this, and I have come to the following conclusion. As the representative of Christ and his Church, I am obliged to give you my decision. Starting at this moment and from now on, I absolutely forbid you to take back even one recruit for your group. No matter who she is, or how worthy she may be, or how much she may beg and plead to come with you, *not one!* Is this clear? Fine, then no further questions or discussion. God will provide. Good day.

And God did provide. Young women from Montreal would continue to enter the ranks in increasing numbers. However, since Marguerite did not know the future, it was with a heavy heart that she left in puzzled dismay and went to visit the two new French communities to study their Rules. Soon it was time to rejoin the travelers bound for New France well before winter set in.

Within weeks after her return to Montreal, the entire Community was shaken by several tragedies, the first on the night of December 6-7, 1683.

"Fire! F-I-R-E!" The dreaded call spread quickly through the building, as did the flames! "Everybody out! Quickly! Grab a blanket, and the towel on the back of your night stand, and move. Check the beds of the girls next to you. If there's any more smoke, put the towel over your mouth and nose — the way we practiced. Big girls, take the hand of a smaller one, and move — right now! Walk quickly, and take slow, deep breaths, the way we practiced. Good, that's right. Keep moving, everyone — follow Sr. Genevieve — I'll be right behind you. Outside as fast as you can — without running."

"It's the Sisters' house! Two are still trapped inside! No, don't try to go in — it's hopeless! Step back! Back! Farther back! The walls are about to cave in. Move back! Quick, everybody — move back! — across the road!"

"Here, take this blanket. You'll freeze just standing in this ice and snow. The fire must have spread in a matter of minutes! It all happened so fast! No, we don't know how it started. Yes, all the boarders are safe and accounted for, and the sisters too — except for Sr. Sommillard and Sr. du Rosoy. Maybe a beam fell on them — we don't know. They must've been caught trying to get everyone else out, or maybe trying to save the records. Such fine, responsible women!"

"Parents, please, find your children and take them home — but be sure to check in with the warden and tell him what you're doing. Other adults, please, take a child or two to your own home — and again, tell the warden, so he can keep his lists straight. Over here — he's over here."

"Poor Sister Marguerite! Her own niece buried in this inferno! And poor Sister Catherine Sommillard — losing her dear older sister! Unbelievable! The two most promising of all the young sisters — gone!"

The residence, the offices, the chapel, the storehouse — all the supplies for winter, everything! Lost — everything lost!

The entire town mourned for days — for weeks. Christmas was almost overshadowed by sadness that year. This had been the large house that Marguerite had so reluctantly built, feeling that it was too large for their needs. "If the Lord does not build the house...." Yet despite her keen sorrow, she was able to face the task of rebuilding, this time — somehow — with energy and confidence.

Nor were these two the only sisters in the young community to die. Within the next decade they would lose five more, three of them in their twenties. Still, life went on, and growth continued.

One of the works dear to Marguerite's heart was a school that her group had opened for young women who had finished their formal schooling but still needed training in "honest trades" — work skills to earn their living. *La Providence* was well named — God's way, through the Congregation, of preparing these women to be the backbone of the colony. Within a few years this school would have to close, surely another difficult decision for Marguerite.

First, however, a completely unexpected event would plunge Marguerite's soul into darkness for more than four years. Sr. Tardy, a sister with whom she lived, began to give her "messages" from a deceased sister, telling her that she, Marguerite, was in a state of eternal damnation and *must* resign. This continued month after month, almost convincing Marguerite that her own sins and infidelities were the cause of all these recent calamities — war with the English, raids by the Iroquois, another tragic fire, fiscal disasters and deaths of young members of the Congregation. When she asked to be relieved of her position as leader, the bishop refused. Marguerite had nowhere to turn — except, as always, to Mary.

What she did not know at the time of this sister's "visions" was this: they were part of a plot by three clerics to reorganize the three religious communities into one. One of these clerics, of course, was to be its superior, therefore making it necessary to remove the present leaders. This plot finally came to light, and after four long years, Marguerite was once more at peace. The "visionary" returned to France, as did the three priests involved.

Marguerite was now 73. When she again asked to resign — no doubt completely worn out by this ordeal, her request was accepted. As often happens, the leader who was elected to take over was, in some ways, very different from Marguerite, especially in temperament, and the oldest member of the new administration was 33. Although Marguerite was given a special fifth position in this new council, she felt as if her opinions no longer mattered. Perhaps she was experiencing the difficulty of no longer being in charge. Perhaps. But she was determined to hold fast to her vision of the Congregation — which she knew in her heart was Mary's gift to her and her sisters.

Yet another crisis awaited her, one that would nearly destroy all that she had worked for since God had first planted the seed within her young heart.

As Bishop Laval aged, an intelligent and enthusiastic young French cleric had been named Vicar General and later became Bishop. A devout ascetic, Bishop Saint-Vallier was, however, also known to be unpredictable and temperamental, making his own decisions without consulting others.

A startling example of this occurred when, in 1694, he presented the Congregation with their new Rule — which *he* had written. Within its pages were some of the original tenets that Fr. Gendret had included back in Troyes, but the many additions taken from the Rule of the cloistered Ursuline Sisters in Quebec would be impossible for Marguerite's group to follow while still being true to their own spirit. According to this new Rule, those who wished to become members in Marguerite's congregation would have to pay a dowry, a condition to which Marguerite herself was utterly opposed. From the very beginning she had made it clear that she wished to accept young women who had all the necessary qualities but could not become religious for lack of money. One of her early biographers stated that Marguerite "cared so little for riches that she would go and carry on her shoulders... a woman who could not even afford to clothe herself but had good will and a true vocation." (Montgolfier, *La vie de la vénérable soeur Marguerite Bourgeoys dite du saint sacrement*, pp. 123-4, quoted in Simpson, *Marguerite Bourgeoys and the Congregation of Notre Dame, 1665-1700*, p. 111)

Even more disturbing about this Rule was what was missing — not a single reference to their desire to emulate the life of Mary, who was not cloistered, but went wherever she was needed to help others.

Moreover, the sisters would be taking *solemn* vows — a term almost synonymous with being cloistered religious. Finally, the addition of a vow of obedience to the local bishop would have made it easier for him to send the sisters wherever he wished, without consulting the Congregation leaders. *Not* good.

In trusting faith Marguerite waited for God's help, but she also acted — speaking out clearly, and sending word to another priest in France who understood her original goal and purpose. The lines were drawn. The "discussions" would last for four years.

10

Soft Rain and Sunshine

Marguerite at market-day in Ville-Marie

$\mathcal{B}$y this time, with gentle moisture and plenty of sun, the young plant had certainly produced at least one of its first flowers, and Marguerite's was a daisy. Why a daisy? Is there any lovely roadside blossom more hardy, more ubiquitous? Is there any more perfect to edge the rest of a garden than this one — tall and slender, nodding in gentle breezes, framing the more elegant roses and showy mums? Besides, Marguerite's very name is the French word for our "daisy"!

Simply reading Marguerite's words, however, might sometimes lead us to conclude that she was over-serious or unfeeling. Missing are her facial expressions, as are her tone of voice and gestures. So consider this: like other good teachers, Marguerite must have been a great story-teller — animated, alive in her whole being — eyes dancing, with legs akimbo or arms waving! Take, for example, her advice to her sisters about being as "unpretentious as pumpkins." This may well have been accompanied by a cheery pointing towards her own portly shape — if she was, or towards that of someone more rotund — along with a caring shoulder-hug. (All this, of course, long before our own era of "Thin Is In.")

The wise words on the pages of Marguerite's writing may also be missing the self-deprecating, good-humored asides that made them more real and palatable. She certainly knew how to laugh at herself and the predicaments she got herself into.

What did she say, for example, when she realized, as the ship sailed down the St. Lawrence, that her satchel had been left behind in Quebec? It is highly unlikely that she folded her hands, raised her eyes to heaven and sighed serenely, "Thy will be done." Did this practical woman grit her teeth and silently chide herself, "Why didn't you just hold onto it your*self*?!"

Or later in France when she was told by Bishop Laval that she was not to take back with her even one recruit, did she shake her head and mutter (*à la* Teresa of Avila), "Lord, if this is the way you treat your friends, it's no wonder you have so few!"? Most probably, Marguerite was usually mature enough to be at peace in the depths of her heart, both with herself and with the world around her, no matter how turbulent the surface. We'll never know.

However, what we do know is that, from the time she experienced Mary's smile during the Rosary procession when she was twenty, Marguerite's motivation — the *why* of all she did, was love. We know this not only from the indisputable evidence of her life, but also from her own words.

Marguerite was keenly aware of Mary's place among the Apostles in the Upper Room at Pentecost, urging her sisters to remember the Spirit's role in their own lives. She reminded them that when the Spirit finds our souls prepared, he can set them afire with His love! (*Writings*, pp. 60-61). Her words reflect the fire that filled her own heart and overflowed to those around her.

Recalling her many encounters with Ville-Marie families, she gave her community another simple reminder: "The sisters ought always to live in the presence of God, like a loving mother who never takes her eyes off her child" (*Writings*, p. 73).

When Marguerite lost her mother as a teenager, did she take the time — or *have* the time — to grieve? Two years later, at age twenty, perhaps she was still feeling the void in her life when Mary's smile touched her heart. She would have been more than ready to receive another mother's warmth and affection.

And surely her relationship with her own father was the wellspring for her lifelong response to God as to a loving father: "Lord, we come to you as children come to the tenderest of fathers" (*Writings*, p. 135). In dealing with those who had not been blessed with this type of relationship with their fathers, Marguerite might have guided them too to a similar response. Perhaps she suggested that they prayerfully consider the attitudes which they *wished* their own fathers had shown towards them, as well as the ways that they *wished* they had been able to respond. She could then help them work through their pain and woundedness, as they yearned for a father who loved them unconditionally, till they found him at last — in God!

Throughout her writings Marguerite most frequently refers to "the Blessed Virgin," Mary's traditional title. Her prayers, however, sometimes begin with the more filial "My good Mother" or "Our Lady and our Mother." Even the more formal titles that she also used, "O most holy Virgin" or "Holy Mother of God," seem, in context, to come from the depths of her heart. In her private conversations with Mary, did she simply call Mary — as some do, "Mom"?

Rarely did Marguerite speak or write directly of her own prayer experiences. In the following metaphor she may come closest to doing so: "It seems to me that we are charcoal ready to be kindled, and that Holy Communion is entirely suited to set us on fire" (*Writings*, p. 204). For her, the Eucharistic union with Jesus, Word made Flesh and Bread of Life, was one which, like a burning flame, "fired all the way to the center..." (*Writings*, p. 204).

Marguerite — sharp businesswoman, community organizer, religious innovator, grief and marriage counselor, intrepid traveler, mother to many, teacher, friend — *and* mystic! Her words are clear: "It is only the love of a lover that penetrates the heart of God" (*Writings*, p. 58).

Soft rain and bright sunshine — so essential for growth! And when both touched the small plant at the same time, no doubt Marguerite was surprised with a glorious rainbow!

11

"Unless the Seed..."

Profession of vows by the Sisters of the Congrégation de Notre-Dame

$\mathcal{M}$arguerite had trusted that if it was the will of God, her dream would endure. Like a good gardener, she knew that, in order to give new life, the seed must die but would live on in this new growth. The painful "discussions" concerning the Rule continued across the Atlantic, since Bishop Saint-Vallier had been recalled to France on several matters. With communications limited to letters carried on ships, the process was slow-moving.

Finally, in the spring of 1698, the bishop met with the Congregation leaders and gave them the revised Rule. Although disappointed with the glaring omission of points they had specifically requested, and the inclusion of others they had asked to be removed, they were able to accept the revision. The 33 members now had their Rule, and were approved as a congregation within the Church — the Church which they truly wished to serve.

The following day the sisters pronounced their vows publicly during Mass, each one adding, after her own name, the name of a saint or a religious mystery important in her life. Because of her devotion to Christ in the Eucharist, Marguerite had chosen to become "Sister Marguerite of the Blessed Sacrament." Her life's work nearly complete, she settled down to a quiet routine of retirement.

Several months later, however, Sr. Catherine Charly, the novice-director, was seriously ill and close to death — and only 33 years old! Marguerite was alarmed at the news!

Catherine was like a granddaughter to her, since on Marguerite's first voyage to Ville-Marie, Catherine's mother, then a yound girl, had been entrusted to her care and had lived with Marguerite until she married. Again, the Woman of Action acted.

Marguerite's spontaneous prayer was overheard by someone nearby. She simply asked God to take her life instead, since Catherine was still much needed in the congregation, whereas she herself was useless.

Evidently God heard this straightforward request from this practical woman and long-standing friend. Catherine began to improve, while Marguerite began to decline steadily. During the next twelve days, she suffered indescribable pain and burning fever, until on January 12 of the new century Marguerite died peacefully, surrounded by her community.

The entire city mourned her death but also celebrated her new life, knowing she was with God whose loving dream she had lived so well. And today, centuries later, we might echo their thoughts as we pray:

Saint Marguerite of Canada,
now bathed in eternal light, immersed in God's own being
yet still filled with compassion for our world,
help us as we, like you, fight the enemy — ignorance,
especially our own, but others' too.
Help us, like you, to understand.
Amen.

12

The Garden

The Sisters are welcomed to a new mission.

*M*arguerite must have been a good gardener, fully aware of the need for patience. As we have seen, it was not until two years before her death that Marguerite's small group received permission to become the first non-cloistered religious congregation in North America. She had trusted that if it was the will of God, her dream would endure — and it did.

She had come to what would become Montreal, one of the largest cities of Canada, to form a new Christian community and to teach the children, especially the girls, who at this time in history were not always educated. What would Marguerite say about our own world, where many girls are still not allowed to go to school and better their lives, where women and children now make up 80% of those living in poverty? Half of our world's children — one billion! — now live in poverty. In fact, millions of women and children spend several hours each day in the tedious but essential task of collecting water. Because of culture or conflict, 57 million children have no access to education. In such a world, Marguerite, who worked both for and with women and children, is indeed close to us.

Marguerite's garden, the Congregation of Notre Dame of Montreal, is still flourishing, still working to address these needs, truly a witness to the power of God alive and well in our midst. Over the centuries, Congregation leaders were also aware, like good horticulturists, that a pot — or a plot

— can be too small, causing the plant to become root bound, and that many plants simply stop growing when they have filled the size of their pot. Between 1932 and 1981, these leaders responded in faith and trust to requests — usually of foreign bishops — to open distant missions. The garden has now spread to eight countries on four continents.

In an excerpt from Marguerite's own writings, we see that she too envisioned her community as a thriving garden:

> I compare this Community to a square in a large garden. For all Christendom is a great garden created by God, and all the communities are as so many plots in this large garden.... The Sisters of the Congregation are as so many plants which occupy one of these squares in the garden.
>
> (*Writings*, p. 63)

Having embraced the King's Wards and so many others in Ville-Marie, Marguerite must be delighted that the Associate program is now flourishing too. More than 900 Associates, women and men who wish to share our Visitation spirituality and be part of our outreach-to others, now join us in ministering to God's people in Cameroon, Canada, Central America, France, Japan and the U.S. To read more about this program, visit our website (cnd-m.org).

All of us are first and foremost Christians, and, as "CNDs," our way of answering our baptismal call is religious life. In these times of uncertainty and lack of accep-

tance by many, apostolic religious life is exciting and challenging. We are learning in a new way that we are women
of the Church, called to love that Church even though, like
ourselves, it is not yet all that Christ is calling it to be. As a
pilgrim people on a journey, we are learning wisdom from
fellow pilgrims. We are becoming better listeners, grounded
in a sense of our humanity, and embracing realistic dialogue
about the Church and its evolving mission. Like Marguerite,
we sometimes have only one answer: compassion!

Society can flourish efficiently and effectively only if
its women are happy and healthy. They will then take care
of their children, so they too can flourish. Marguerite knew
this, and we, Sisters and Associates, are trying to live her
vision, reaching out as Mary did to the needs of our world,
living the Good News of Jesus in our time as she lived it
in hers. We are doing this especially through all forms of
education in faith and justice, as well as through social net-
working and nonviolent actions in our own milieu.

However, as in other religious communities, the sisters
of the Congregation in this garden are now less numerous
than they were during the historical anomaly of the post-
World War II high in the U.S. and Canada. In a Church
that has opened up to women many other opportunities for
ministry, fewer now apply to religious communities. If you
are interested in learning how *you* might find a home *and* a
fascinating ministry/career within our Church and among
our members — from Belgium, Cameroon, Canada, El Salva-

dor, France, Guatemala, Honduras, Japan, Trinidad and the U.S., go to the same site (cnd-m.org).

As Cardinal Suhard, archbishop of Paris during World War II, said, "Being a witness to Christ means... that we are living a mystery. It means living in such a way that our life would not make sense if God did not exist" (Suhard, *Priests Among Men*, 1949). We have come to realize that the life to which we were called is more challenging than we had first envisioned, but also far more rewarding than we had ever imagined!

Speaking with Marguerite...

Now that you have met Marguerite, you may wish to speak with her about her life, and about yours. Parts of the following may spark your own thoughts and prayers to this loving woman. Sit back. Relax. Take a long, slow breath and, as you read these words to Marguerite, your new friend, make them your own — or adapt them, and smile!

You walk with us in dangers sensed,
    and unsuspected in the dark,
    beyond the known, approved, expected —
    to find God in our heartbeats and our dreams.
With you we turn to continents uncharted,
    to hovels, barrios, wasteland suburbs,
to troubled, voiceless, shackled minds,
    to haunted, hollow eyes on nightly news.

You walk with us on paths outside the fort
    of safe success.
With you we follow Mary, not in austerity, penance,
    or constant contemplation (where once you too
        felt drawn), but in simple journeys —
each day a Visitation, where women bring the dawn
    in song and grateful praise,

and hidden service frees for future greatness,
    where new life greets our own in joy!

We laugh — an echo of your own,
    with friends of vibrant years —
    Jeanne Mance or faithful Paul.
What else but laugh at memories of salt-sprayed sleep
    pillowed on a coil of rope!
How else survive the birth pangs of a strange new venture,
    but laugh and shrug your shoulders?
How else convince our News is truly Good
    except with joy — deep and lasting joy!

Mending, baking, scrubbing, soothing —
    no task too big, or small, for mother-hands.
A mattress or a remedy, a handclasp or a hug —
    you sensed the need, and gave.
You nourished hungers of the spirit too with solid fare —
    bread and soup, well-seasoned with wit, lively or
    profound, and shared the recipe with all who asked.

Truly present to the gentle and the grumbling,
    the sniffles, triumphs, dry tears of others,
    may we too listen, and respond.
Our stable walls have also stretched in welcome
    to a family unforeseen: to daughters of the King,
    and sons, the young with eager questions
and not-so-young with hardened answers, to children
    of the open plains, the ghettos and the mines.

You pray with us to let God be our soil, moisture, seed,
    to let God warm us in the morning shade,
    unfolding petals perfect in their brief brightness!
You speak. We listen gladly.
    Be always little, like cabbages and pumpkins...

Yes! To God be the glory!
   ...at home — like Mary — with shepherds and kings.
Yes! To God be the praise!
   ...and poor. Be poor in spirit, generous and kind,
   for only what we share is truly ours.

But our needs have grown;
   their tendrils choke our freedom.
Pity our weakness. Pity our chains.
   Pity our part with tyrants'
   guilt, who strip and starve God's other children,
   close their hearts, and smiling, turn away.
Give us your eyes to see the chasm of our nothingness!
   Come closer, you say.
We feel another darkness, a limitless abyss far deeper
   than the misery of stark need, or creature poverty —
   a Father's mercy, a Mother's love.

Marguerite, in us you live your vision.
   Through us you touch our world.
You've taught us well. You've shown us when to lay aside
   our dream, and waken to another's.

But this one gift surpasses all the rest: Mary, our guide.
   Mary, our life! We feel her smile and bow in wordless
wonder. Then, arms flung wide, we run to her embrace!

Marguerite, woman of action and watchful mother,
   you still love children, women, families!
Help each of us to live God's loving dream for us
   in this, our "one wild and precious life"!

Trusting your love, we dare to ask for one gift more:
   When layered years are gently scraped away,
may God's compassion be complete in us — like you,
   dear mother, mentor, sister, friend!

Bibliography

Writings of Marguerite Bourgeoys: Autobiography and Spiritual Testament. Originally in French; translated by M.V. Cotter, CND. Montreal: Congregation de Notre Dame, 1976.

Simpson, Patricia. *Marguerite Bourgeoys and Montreal, 1640-1665,* Montreal: McGill-Queen's University Press, 1997.

Simpson, Patricia. *Marguerite Bourgeoys and the Congregation of Notre Dame, 1665-1700,* Montreal: McGill-Queen's University Press, 2005.

Suhard, Emmanuel, *Priests Among Men*, Paris/Montreal: Fides, 1949.

Note

In writing this brief biography of Saint Marguerite Bourgeoys, I am deeply indebted to the meticulous and thorough research of Sr. Patricia Simpson, CND. The second half of this short book could virtually be one long series of footnotes, drawing on her definitive (and fascinating!) biography of Marguerite. I cannot recommend these two volumes highly enough. Both are available at our website, cnd-m.org

L.F., CND